Ten Rules for Common "Cents" Investing

BRIAN M. MURPHY

DEDICATION

This book is dedicated to my best friend, counselor, and most ardent supporter for over three decades: my wife Cherie Denise Murphy. Her devotion, wisdom, and love have guided me through many a tough time.

Thanks, baby. You made this all possible.

CONTENTS

ACKNOWLEDGMENTS

Thanks to my lovely bride Cherie and my kids Patrick, Meghan, and Tara, for encouraging me every step of the way.

Thanks to the devoted team at My Pathway whose patience and urging kept me moving forward. To Dr.'s Eugene Fama and Ken French for building the Three Factor Model. To Bryce, for letting me over the fence, and all my friends at DFA for helping me make sense of investing. To Diana for urging me to keep writing and to my many loyal clients for fueling the success of Pathways Financial Partners and My Pathway.

COMMON "CENTS" INVESTMENT RULES

As a financial advisor for three decades, I witnessed some of the strongest bull and toughest bear markets in history. One might think I have seen it all. Smart people in the investment business know that no one ever sees it all. The next bull or bear always lurks around the corner.

I now embrace academic science and proven principles that help manage risk and capture returns. Shifting my investment focus from Wall Street to academia opened my eyes over a decade ago and I hope it will open yours.

I share my journey with the hope of guiding you on yours.

A Few Thoughts to Get Started

Merchants, slave traders and boat captains arriving in the New World over 300 years ago and looking for investors gave birth to "Wall Street." In the beginning, everyone knew the risks of the high seas, lost cargo and bad business deals. Investors, then and now, aim to gain an edge on their peers and a return on their capital. Options, futures, and nearly every financial instrument trading today can trace its roots to this tiny street in New York City.

Nothing is free on Wall Street. The ever-present middleman, working for a fee or a commission, takes a little piece of every trade.

Born in lower Manhattan, Wall Street is the financial capital of the world and the most powerful economic force in history. A mere eight-block section of lower Manhattan, "Wall Street" is now the generic term for the U.S. investment banking industry. I intend to open your eyes to the complex and conflicting motives behind Wall Street's operations.

The United States of America was born on Wall Street. George Washington took the presidential oath of office on the Federal Hall balcony at Wall and Nassau Streets in 1789. The first Congress, Supreme Court, and Executive Branch offices were housed there as well. America's economy, modern-day investment banking, and the world's most sophisticated and transparent capital markets were born on this tiny street with a church at one end and a graveyard on the other.

Wall Street endures as the center of global finance in spite of countless recessions, Civil war, the Great Depression, and devastation of 9-11. Capitalism traces its roots to Scotland, but this tiny patch of real estate lays claim to its meteoric rise over the last three centuries.

I grew up in New Jersey and could see the lights of lower Manhattan from my bedroom window on a clear night. When I was a young boy my father worked in the Woolworth building just a few blocks from Wall Street. My own grandfather, the son of Irish immigrants and a first-generation NYC fire captain, fought ferocious fires in this eclectic corner of the world over one hundred years ago. Now it's filled with restaurants, fish markets, giant piers adjacent to heliports, skyscrapers, and concrete canyons filled with businesses large and small. I am proud of my heritage, proud to be a financial advisor, and proud to be an American.

Individual investors need to be savvy and well informed to compete against a myriad of institutional traders, algorithms, dark pools and hedge funds. The simple principles that drive successful investing are not part of mainstream thinking around Wall Street. They are antithetical to Wall Street's thinking but nonetheless true.

The truth is clear: simple, common sense investing trumps more expensive and complex strategies almost all the time. As a professional financial advisor for three decades I've learned quite a bit about people and investing. My mom used to say experience is what you get when you get what you don't want. I look forward to sharing knowledge gained from experience in the pages ahead.

Based on common sense, this book offers 10 simple rules to help you succeed with personal investing. You will learn more about how stocks and bonds work while refining your knowledge of capital markets. I hope you will open your mind to the truth of evidence based investing.

RULE #1
DON'T TRY TO BEAT THE MARKET

The Birth of an Index

Costs, in the form of fees and commissions, are how the Wall Street crowd turns your money into their money. One of my heroes, John Bogle, founder of Vanguard often states "the return of all investors is the return of the market minus costs." Costs are the lifeblood of Wall Street and, quite often, the bane of individual investors. Costs are well disguised, unclear, and frequently conveyed in print too small to read.

In 1884, Charles H. Dow began tracking 11 publicly traded companies, mostly railroads. He began recording individual stock values and tracking their daily average prices. This created the first stock market index. Dow's simple method became a powerful global standard that survives to this day.

In the early days, Dow's calculations became a "convenient benchmark" for analyzing stock prices. Known today as the Dow Jones Industrial Average, "The Dow," now contains 30 stocks from diverse U.S. industries. The Dow endures as viable gauge of economic activity and investor sentiment in the United States and across the globe.

The Standard and Poor's 500 Index, includes 500 companies reflecting a broad cross-section of the U.S. economy. It stands as a better-diversified benchmark for investors to track than the Dow. The S&P 500 is the "one to beat" for most U.S. stock funds and managers. Attempting to outperform the S&P 500 can be costly and difficult. It is a fact that the vast majority of professional and individual investors fail to outperform this simple index.

If you ponder this truth for just a moment, it makes perfect sense. The return of all investors is the market's return minus all fees and costs. Inevitably, the return for most investors must be less than the market. How can this be true? Too many investors pay high fees and commissions with a blind disregard for the impact on returns.

Beating the Market is No Easy Task

There are over 25,000 mutual funds, including open end, closed end, and Exchange Traded Funds (ETF'S). That number expands every month with ETFs growing in popularity with investors. Most investors are unaware that the majority of funds fail to beat basic indexes. If you doubt this, do a quick web search for the term: SPIVA. SPIVA is an acronym for a public database called Standard and Poor's Indices Versus Active.

Simply stated, SPIVA tracks raw data on how funds perform and report that data to the public on their website. SPIVA data goes back more than ten years. Most mainstream financial advisors are unaware of, or choose to ignore the truth behind this data. The statistics reveal that most stock and bond fund managers fail to beat their basic benchmark. They fail in bull markets and bear markets, and they fail most of the time. In spite of persistent failure, many funds collect hefty fees while investing your money.

The facts are shocking. Over long periods of time like five and ten years, more than 80% of large-cap funds fail to beat the S&P 500 Index. When it comes to bonds, the statistics are more astonishing and disappointing. Over five and ten years periods, the failure rate is above 80% and for government bond funds the failure rate is above 90%. For investors and fund managers alike, it's just too hard to overcome the hurdle presented by fees.

The data reveals that beating market indexes is impossible for most fund managers. Investing in mutual funds is not an endeavor where you always get what you pay for. According to research behemoth

Morningstar—the best predictor of fund performance is fees. Funds with high fees are far more likely to under-perform their lower fee counterparts.

The moral of the story is simple: Don't attempt to beat the market with high-cost, actively managed funds. It's a waste of your time and your money.

RULE #2
DIVERSIFY AROUND THE GLOBE

Investors are wise to own stocks in companies outside the United States in developed and emerging markets. Diversification can help buffer the downturns and smooth returns over long periods. World market capitalization refers to the total market value of every stock traded around the world.

I began my career in the mid-1980s when the United States represented more 70% of the world's market capitalization. Today, that percentage has fallen to less than 50%, with U.S. stocks representing just under half of the total value.

Think of all the foreign products we consume from companies like Toyota, Samsung, Heineken and so many others. The point is crystal clear. If you ignore foreign markets, you deny yourself access to some of the world's best investments. These firms make some of the world's best products—and earn handsome profits doing so.

Emerging versus Developed Markets

International markets are divided into two broad categories: "developed" and "emerging." International developed markets include Germany, Japan, Australia, and many others with mature economies. Emerging markets include Poland, Greece, China and others with less developed economies.

Investing in publicly traded stocks of foreign companies presents significant opportunities for U.S. investors. The first decade of the new millennium rewarded emerging market investors more handsomely than U.S. or international developed markets. Even better, these markets often move higher when U.S. markets are declining and can help smooth out returns. More importantly, as investors, we want to earn a return on our money. By investing around the globe, we gain access to returns from great companies whose products we use on a regular basis.

Strategy for Global Investing

How much you should invest in foreign markets is a personal decision best made with the help of a competent financial advisor. Most investors do not have the stomach for an entire portfolio of emerging-markets stocks. These smaller, less liquid, markets often experience dramatic price swings in the direction we don't like: down! More risks with global investing include exposure to different currencies, political drama, and too many more to list here.

But there is a bottom line. If you want access to the growth from some of the world's greatest companies, you must diversify outside the USA. In the long run you stand to increase your return and reduce your risk.

One rule of thumb for global investing is to take a "market neutral" approach. That means investing your portfolio according to the actual weightings of each of the three broad categories: US, international, and emerging markets. This creates wider swings in value and exceeds the patience and the risk tolerance of the average investor.

My approach is to look at the percentage of a portfolio committed to stocks and break it down as if investing a single dollar bill. For every dollar invest 70 cents in the U.S., 20 cents in international, and 10 cents in emerging markets. There is no magic in this. It's a simple, diversified strategy best deployed with low-cost ETF's and index funds.

Diversification is a powerful tool for increasing return and lowering risk. Spreading your portfolio around the world provides access to returns from great global companies.

RULE #3
KEEP COSTS LOW

Massachusetts Investors Trust began operations as
the first open end mutual fund in the United States in
1924. It survives to this day as part of MFS Investment
Management. According to recent data, there are more
than 25,000 mutual funds available to U.S. investors.
Open-end, closed-end, exchange-traded, inverse,
leveraged, stock, bond, balanced, lifestyle, commodity,
long-short, target-date, international, and emerging-
market funds to name a few. Investors can even own
"frontier-markets" investing in Jamaica, United Arab
Emirates, and Kenya among others. With so many
funds to choose from, selecting the right mix is harder
today than it's ever been.

The concept of mutual funds is simple. Like-minded
investors pool their money together gaining instant
diversification while pursuing a common goal. Mutual
funds provide investors large and small access to a

broad range of stocks or bonds within a single vehicle. Mutual Funds are perhaps the most powerful concepts in the history of investing. Countless investors benefit today and have for decades.

Active versus Passive Funds

A quick peek in the Wall Street Journal or an on line financial site reveals the wide range of costs charged by mutual fund companies. All funds fall into one of two simple categories labeled as either "active" or "passive." Active funds seek to beat the market. Managers of these funds believe they can add value above their fees and will outperform a market index. Passive funds track the return of a specific index and have lower fees on average than their active counterparts.

Active funds aim for specific objectives by investing in stocks or bonds. An appropriate index for comparison is almost always available for this type of fund. Think of the many "growth" and "balanced" funds as examples, with their objective stated right in the fund name. Many large-company growth funds measure themselves against the S&P 500 Index.

Passive funds, on the other hand, simply mimic the performance of a specific index. That's it. No fluff and no extra fees. Index funds are low cost, tax efficient and simple to understand.

If you think about it, there is little point in owning a fund that seeks to beat a benchmark yet fails to do so.

Why Beating Mr. Market is Tough

A good example of a hard-to-beat benchmark is the NASDAQ 100 Index. This index includes 100 of the largest U.S. companies many of which are tech firms. You can invest in the NASDAQ 100 via an ETF with the trading symbol QQQ. Often referred to as the "qubes" by your favorite financial commentators, QQQ is one of the largest and best known of all ETF's. The cost of owning QQQ is reasonable as it carries an annual expense of .20%, or what financial jargon refers to as "20 basis points."

The most popular benchmark in the US, the S&P 500 Index, is available to investors in many different forms. One of the best and most popular is via the Vanguard ETF with the symbol VOO. Its expense ratio is only .05% or, as you may have surmised, 5 basis points.

I find this astonishing and you should, too. Remember the Massachusetts Investors Trust mentioned earlier? According the fund's prospectus, the up-front commission for buying this fund could be as high as 5.75%! Fund research giant Morningstar reports the current annual cost of holding this fund is .70% (70 basis points). Yes, that is correct and not a misprint. Annual management fees are ten times more than the similar offering from Vanguard.

Oh, one more thing. Since inception in September of 2010, VOO has outperformed MFS's Investors Trust. There is no guarantee this trend will go on forever. A quick Internet search will verify current performance and resolve any doubts.

The intent is not to single out MFS as a fund family or Massachusetts Investors Trust. Rather, it's to make a key point using the oldest, most venerable fund illustrating just how hard it is to beat "Mr. Market." To pay more than 10 times in annual fees for one fund over another without getting a higher return is impossible to justify.

In all fairness to the folks at MFS Investors Trust, its annual fee is not extreme among so-called active funds. But as investors, we must ask ourselves if we are getting the best bang for our buck. Most of the time, the answer is "No!"

More Evidence

Morningstar reports that in 2014 the average Vanguard investor paid investment management fees of $0.18 for every $100 invested while active fund investors paid an average of $1.24 on the same $100. * (WSJ 1-5-15). Simple arithmetic is impossible to deny. The game of trying to beat the market is costly and difficult.

As an institutional consultant I fought the truth for a long time. Selecting active managers capable of beating their benchmark for long periods is tough. Over time, the overwhelming evidence led to my surrendering the truth. Success among active managers is often luck and not skill. Identifying winners in advance is a loser's game.

A Closer Look at Indexing

Let's take a closer look at index funds.

Remember the story of Charles H. Dow, who designed his "market basket" to track the data behind the movement of stock prices? It turns out Mr. Dow pioneered a simple yet powerful concept. Creating an index is more than a great source of data; it's also an excellent communication and investment tool. Buy a basket of diverse companies, reinvest dividends and you will beat 90% of all investors. From the Dow Jones Industrial Index grew many more indexes. Many are more diverse, less volatile, and better performing than the Dow.

Standard and Poors, Russell, Barclays and others take a thoughtful, disciplined approach index construction. Companies that comprise an index typically change no more than once per calendar year. This static approach gives index funds a cost advantage over active competitors trying to beat the market. This compelling edge for index funds shows up in two key arenas: tax efficiency and trading costs.

With minimal or no trading in any given year, index funds end up being tax efficient. Investing in an index fund means you may own many of the same companies for decades resulting in lower turnover and taxes along the way. With any mutual fund, the responsibility for paying taxes passes through to the end investor. Index funds often result in lower taxes than active funds. Active funds tend toward more buying and selling activity—also known as "turnover"—than index funds. Fewer buys and sells of stocks and bonds results in lower trading costs and lower taxes for index fund investors.

By now, the picture should be clear. Low-cost, tax-efficient index funds tend to deliver higher returns than active funds. Active funds have an uphill climb with higher turnover, trading costs, and taxes along the way.

Avoiding Pirates and the Pit of Poor Returns

Try explaining the concept of active versus passive investing to your kids, and the point becomes clear. On one hand, a set of investors is continually trying to beat the competition. It's like watching the pole vault competition at the Olympic Games. Each competitor is like a fund manager or individual investor trying to fly higher than the competition every year.

But pole-vaulting competitors have foam-filled pits to break their fall. The pit of poor returns fills up with active managers seeking higher returns and falling short. Bad decisions, high turnover and high fees become insurmountable for active managers. It is nearly impossible to keep up with their index brethren.

Remember Bernie Madoff and the tragedy that happened to his clients? In one of the biggest scams of all time, Madoff's clients lost billions. They would have been far better off accepting the return of the S&P 500 instead of buying into the false promise of high returns.

My prospective clients often walk in disgruntled and disillusioned by a mainstream financial advisor. We refer to the scurrilous advisors as "pirates." Why pirates, you may ask? Aren't they the guys who board your vessel on a long journey and steal your precious cargo? Enough said.

The first step in our wealth management process is what we refer to as a "discovery meeting." We learn about where prospective clients have come from and where they'd like to go. We review their tax returns, their financial account statements, their mortgage statements, etc. This helps us determine where they are on their financial journey and how we can best help them.

Often clients' portfolios include money managers and mutual funds approved by a major broker dealer. It is common for fees to be high with performance well below that of major stock and bond indexes. It's like a pirate guiding you along journey and pilfering your wealth. Modern-day financial pirates are slicker than in previous centuries, but the effect is the same.

Think of Captain Jack Sparrow in the classic film Pirates of the Caribbean. He was always after what he wanted, and if you were lucky, you got a little bit of what you wanted by joining him on his journey. But it was always a risky proposition from beginning to end. Many clients describe their former advisor as a "nice person " but they "had trouble making good returns." Wasn't Captain Jack a charming guy as well?

The investing pattern for pirates is predictable and pathetic. They use algorithms, sector rotation, market timing, momentum, back-tested and dynamic trading strategies. They have more tricks than Captain Jack and his entire crew. Over the long term, these strategies are more likely to benefit your advisor and his firm more than you and your family.

The more you pay for fund management, the lower your expected return. Ignore flashy ads and "superior" recent performance. Over the long run, you are better off using a lower-cost approach. Read the fine print and be especially careful to ignore claims of back tested strategies that seem too good to be true. Investing is like life; if it sounds too good to be true, it probably is.

RULE #4
KEEP BONDS SHORT

Bonds may be the simplest of all investments and one of the least understood. Bonds are like loaning money, only you are loaning to a company or government rather than an individual. When you buy a bond or bond fund you are loaning money to an issuer like Apple or the US Treasury. Bonds pay investors a stated rate of interest for a specific period of time. Like other securities, bonds can be purchased individually or through a mutual fund or ETF.

Invest in a bond fund and gain the benefits of diversification and forego the feature of a fixed value at maturity. Bonds appear simpler and easy to understand but have become more complex in recent times. Mortgage-backed securities are an intricate and well-known hybrid. Mortgage backed bonds were a key catalyst for the collapse of world financial markets in 2008–2009. Rather than analyze the countless hybrids, we will focus on one of the better ways for most investors to own bonds.

For individual investors, bonds have two primary roles in a portfolio: stability and income.

Individual bonds may come due or "mature" over many different time frames. Short-term bonds issued by the US Treasury are often called T-Bills. Longer maturity bonds are can mature thirty or even forty years from today.

TIPS, the inflation adjusted form of US Treasury bonds were born a little over a decade ago. The acronym "TIPS" stands for Treasury Inflation Protected Securities. TIPS aim to protect investors from the negative impact of inflation. They pay a stated rate of interest for a fixed period. Unlike traditional bonds, TIPS can add principal value at maturity if the inflation rate rises over the life of the bond.

The Teeter-Totter of Bonds & Interest Rates

While bonds appear as the safest of investments, they still carry risks. The two big inherent risks are 1) the risk of losing purchasing power posed by inflation and 2) the risk of losing principal.

Principal risk comes about in two ways. First, the issuer can get into financial trouble. Second, higher interest rates in the future can reduce a bonds market value if you go to sell. If a company goes bankrupt, bond investors can lose their entire investment. Bond investor claims are ahead of stock investors claims in a bankruptcy. When interest rates rise, current bond prices tend to fall.

Price movements relative to interest rates can be a tough concept for many investors. For decades, I've used the analogy of the teeter-totter. Picture at one end of the teeter-totter the bond you own and at the other end current interest rates. When you invest in a bond, both ends of the plank are level. Interest rates are the heavyweights in this game and always dictate where the current price of the bond stands. When interest rates go up, the current price of your bond must go down. Conversely, when interest rates go down, the price of your bond must go up. It's a relatively simple concept to envision.

The Downside of Long-Term Bonds

It is easier to comprehend bond price movements when you envision how investors get paid for taking risks. Bonds seem like they are safe investments and are exactly that most of the time. The big danger for a bond's value is when interest rates go up. Bonds maturing many years in the future become less valuable when interest rates rise. Imagine holding a bond that comes due in 10 years currently paying you a return of 2%. If inflation shows up and current 10-year rates rise to 3%, your bond will immediately lose value in the marketplace. An investor who wants your bond would demand the 3% yield currently available on new 10-year bonds. In the market your bond price will fall to provide the new investor the same yield available on new issue bonds.

Based on a 2% yield and a $10,000 investment, you would receive $200 per year on your investment. Unfortunately, if rates rise, a newly issued version of your bond would pay investors $300 per year. That's 50% more per year than you are currently receiving. To receive the same 3%, or $300, from your bond, an investor would be willing to pay you only 90% of your original investment. In other words, you would need to discount the price by 10% for a new investor to step in and buy your bond.

This example is an oversimplification but it is accurate. The new investor demands a lower price to generate that extra $100 per year in income she requires. With trading desks operating 24/7, trades now happen in milliseconds and computers determine prices.

Longer bonds can be more complex and risky. It makes sense for most of us to own bonds with short to intermediate-term maturities. Long-term bonds are most appropriate for long-term investors. Pension plans and insurance companies with never-ending future needs should own long bonds.

The Tradeoff's of Bond Investing

Quarterly: 1964-2010

Not all investors embrace risk as expressed by standard deviation. Long-term bonds are appropriate for some investors.

Historically, longer-maturity bonds have higher standard deviations and more inherent risks than shorter-maturity bonds.

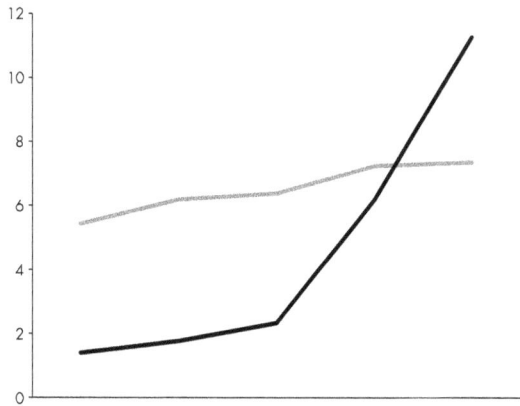

Maturity	One-Month US Treasury Bills	Six-Month US Treasury Bills	One-Year US Treasury Notes	Five-Year US Treasury Notes	Twenty-Year US Treasury Bonds
Annualized Compound Return (%)	5.45	6.20	6.41	7.27	7.37
Annualized Standard Deviation (%)	1.42	1.77	2.34	6.21	11.29

This chart is helpful when trying to understand the risks and rewards of investing in short-term, intermediate-term, and long-term U.S. Government Bonds. Long-term bonds tend to reward investors with higher returns but carry higher risk to principal than short-term bonds. Remember, higher interest rates in the future pose big risks for bond investors.

RULE #5
FAVOR SMALL & VALUE STOCKS

Investing is fundamentally about risk, reward, and the tradeoffs between the two. Take more risk and expect more return. Sounds simple, yet scores of investors fail to recognize this fundamental principle.

Persistent patterns appear when examining financial markets returns over long time frames. Over periods of 20 years or longer, truths begin emerging. Stocks beat bonds, value investing beats growth investing, and small stocks beat large stocks. There is one huge caveat: investing in stocks is not like punching a time clock. Returns in all investments vary a good deal from one year to the next. Returns from stocks are not sequential and so investing requires patience. Smaller, more value-oriented companies provide higher returns to disciplined investors who stay the course. Successful investing requires tenacity. Small value stocks provide higher returns only to disciplined investors who stay the course. The reward for owning smaller companies may take many years to pay off. History strongly suggests following this well-worn path will pay off.

Patience and the Game of Risk

What all this means to investors is that small and value stocks carry more risk yet provide higher returns over long periods. This book revolves around this truth: small-value investors reap greater rewards over time. All investors need do is tilt their portfolio in favor of small and value stocks and wait . . . and wait . . . and wait. By accepting higher risk, you will earn a superior return.

Larger, established companies tend to have reliable sales, revenues, dividends, and earnings. Investors who own big companies accept lower returns simply because we are taking less risk. On the flip side, when we invest in smaller companies, we are taking more risk. Remember: Investing is all about risk and reward. Over time, investors make more with small companies, but to achieve that higher return, they take more risk.

What exactly is risk? Where does it come from, and should we avoid it or embrace it? A better question is: Can we avoid risk altogether or can we manage it? Great questions often have simple answers, and the principles that apply to risk are simpler than you might think. Risk is the proverbial double-edged sword that cuts both ways. Lower risk investments have lower expected returns. Higher returns compensate investors for added risks they encounter.

Risk is Not an Abstract Concept

The investment industry defines risk as "standard deviation." Financial advisors like to throw the term volatility around in conjunction with describing risk. Standard deviation measures how spread out a group of numbers are on a graph. A low standard deviation indicates lower less risk. A high standard deviation means the numbers are more dispersed indicating more risk. Ask your broker to define this and he or she may struggle to explain the concept.

I do not define risk with abstract statistical terms, nor should you. Risk to an investor is the ability or likelihood that any investment will lose money. Standard deviation and volatility refer to your chances of losing money or making money. If you are like most investors, you don't mind volatility on the upside, but you despise it on the downside. Try explaining volatility to your kids and you will end up discussing losing money.

Remember, high standard deviation and high volatility are not inherently bad. Risk and return can never be separated. Riskier assets tend to produce higher returns over time. If you avoid risk, you are likely avoiding return. Embracing the risk of stocks and holding on is to embrace their expected returns.

The Question of Risk: A Scenario

My favorite definition of risk is the opportunity and likelihood of losing money over any given period. I like to frame risk with a question. "Mr. and Mrs. Jones, If your $1,000,000 portfolio drops in value to less than $500,000, would you declare me an idiot and search for another advisor?"

Most investors reply, "Absolutely!"

"Good," I say. "Then you can't invest 100% of your money in stocks. The likelihood of losing half your money at some point, even in diversified portfolio, is inevitable." Later I will bring them to a more comfortable place, which is often a loss number closer to 20%.

"A decline from $1,000,000 to, say, $800,000 would not cause you to run screaming into the arms of another advisor? We would ride out the storm together?"

The normal response is usually a slow nod followed by brief eye contact between spouses. Then one of the two will say, "Yes, we think we could handle that type of loss, as long as we were comfortable with your approach."

"Great," I say. "That means you can only invest 40% of your money in the stock market. If you go beyond that amount in stocks, one day you may lose more than you are comfortable losing."

In the stock market, the more time you stay invested, the lower your risk of losing. Unfortunately, "long term" is an abstract concept for many advisors and investors alike. Good advisors understand the data driving returns. Great advisors go one step further keeping clients invested, helping them hang on during bear markets.

Dalbar's Data: Analyzing the Market

It is a well-known and published fact that investors, as a whole, earn less than the available return in financial markets. Dalbar publishes perhaps the best-known study on this, and you will find it at www.dalbar.com. Much like J. D. Powers in the automobile business, Dalbar tracks mutual fund data and returns earned by investors. Dalbar has earned credibility by publishing its findings in a consistent format for over twenty years.

As with all aspects of investing, one must be circumspect when looking at averages and conclusions. Some attack Dalbar's methods but I do not. To me, Dalbar's approach is a valid way of looking at returns earned by all mutual fund investors on an aggregate basis. I agree with Dalbar's conclusions and they tell a sad story.

In Dalbar's own words, its reporting "explains how investors and advisors adapt to market conditions and produce investor returns using investor behaviors, the psychological factors that drive them, and the knowledge of how investment classes have acted in the past." The company's research looks at how money flows into and out of mutual funds and comes to this bleak conclusion. *En masse, investors tend to buy at the top and sell at the bottom.*

Yep, you read that right. Folks get scared when markets correct and go into free-fall. They become greedy and confident when bull markets are long in the tooth. For most investors it's euphoria at the top and capitulation at the bottom. This may be why many investors fear the stock market. Their own behavior leads them to wrong conclusions driven by irrational fears. If you can imagine yourself saying, "I knew I should have put it all in cash" then do not invest in stocks.

The Cabbie and the Tech Boom

Perhaps you are old enough to remember the runaway tech boom and meteoric rise in stock prices during the late 1990s. You may recall the false confidence of pundits and average investors during what we now refer to as the "dot-com bubble."

I recall getting into a cab in New York City in 1999. The cab driver spit out stock tips during the entire ride from La Guardia to lower Manhattan. I asked a few questions and learned he was from Pakistan and had been in the United States for about six years. I am wearing the Wall Street uniform: white shirt, dark suit, and red tie—heading to a meeting with a money management firm in Manhattan. For almost an hour, a cabbie is telling me how he's getting rich by investing in Initial Public Offerings (IPO) of Internet star ups. IPO's like "quepasa.com" to who knows what, had him raking in the dough and eager to share his insights. After an hour with this man hearing about the piles of money he was effortlessly raking in, I knew the market had to be near its peak.

I recall an interesting Warren Buffet interview around that time. Buffet said he was not smart enough to understand companies with no earnings or book value, and little more than a good idea going public with multi-million-dollar market value. I also recall spending a lot of time convincing clients that trees don't really grow to the moon. The lack of rational thought associated with the tech boom points to the over confidence investors tend to feel near a market top. Trees do not grow to the moon and a bust followed the boom. The euphoria ended in late 1999 and three very tough years in U.S. stock markets followed.

Small Value Stocks

Fortunately, I discovered small-value stocks as an asset class earlier in the 1990s. Early in the decade, I began recommending small value funds and managers to all my clients. I never understood the valuations of the tech boom. We avoided much of the decline in tech stocks that followed in 2000–2003. I prefer stocks of companies that have low debt, a higher book value relative to total market value, and solid dividends. Tech stocks in the late '90s offered none of these qualities, so the hoopla never overtook our firm. It is true we missed out on some hefty returns, but we also avoided the catastrophic losses that followed.

It is noteworthy that small-value stocks as an asset class in the United States did not rise along with the tech sector in the late 1990s. According to the Center for Research in Security Prices, small value stocks came raging back after 2000. Between 2000-2005, small value stocks provided patient investors with average returns of 19.6%.

A client fired me as his advisor in late 1999. One of his investments with me, a big-name fund with a solid long-term track record, increased in value that year by only 45%. His personally chosen Fidelity Select Technology fund had more than doubled in value during that one year. He concluded he was more adept at picking funds than me. So he abandoned a disciplined asset allocation approach and invested more money in tech stocks. There are no substitutes for patience and discipline. We can only imagine how it turned out for my client who abandoned his disciplined asset allocation. This small piece of anecdotal evidence shows that investors are most confident at exactly the wrong time.

Ignoring Index Funds is Costly

Dalbar concludes that average investors earn less than 50% of the available return offered by the S&P 500 Index. It is no coincidence that investors buy funds with high fees and high turnover. Index funds from Vanguard, Blackrock and others charge low fees and have low turnover. Investors miss the return of the market by getting in and out and the wrong time. Buying and holding index and evidence based funds is a more compelling approach.

Think of explaining the concept of buying an index fund to your young son or daughter. "Junior, you can buy the whole market cheaper than you can buy the little pieces. And if you just hold on, you'll beat the friends who think they are smarter than you—and pay less in taxes along the way. "

Low cost, tax efficient index funds are ideal for smart, patient investors.

RULE #6

BEWARE TURNOVER, TAXES, AND TIMING

Benjamin Franklin noted more than two centuries ago, "The only two certainties in life are death and taxes." Investors must pay taxes on dividends and realized capital gains while holding a mutual fund. One way or the other, the IRS gets its pound of flesh.

As an investor, you owe taxes on a fund when you sell shares or when your fund realizes a gain from the sale of securities held in its portfolio. Every time your fund manager buys or sells a stock or bond she is creating turnover. Turnover creates more transaction costs for fund shareholders and often leads to more taxes. Turnover always has a cost.

On average, actively managed funds turn over roughly 85% of their holdings each year. Turnover not only drives up trading costs, it often creates tax liability at the same time. A tax bill on a fund that loses money in a given year can be an unwelcome surprise indeed.

The purpose of investing is to earn a positive rate of return. If a fund manager makes a profit on a security, shareholders pay taxes on the gain unless the fund is held in an IRA or 401(k) where taxes are deferred until later. In a taxable account, it is just as important to consider a fund's after-tax return, as it is to consider the return stated in the prospectus.

Remember, index funds tend to generate far less tax liability than active funds, enabling you to keep more of what you make.

Market Timing is Nearly Impossible

"Market Timing" is the attempt by investors to get in an out of the market, often at the wrong time. Remember the Dalbar study discussed in the last rule? Investors are wired for fear and greed. Fear tends to be at its highest when markets are in free fall. And greed tends to jump in when all your friends and relatives are bragging about how much money they're making in the stock market.

Market timing success requires two correct decisions: when to get out and when to get back in. Most market timers claim they can do this with success over and over again. To guess correctly just once, a "timer" has a 50/50 chance of being right. To guess correctly twice, the odds drop to 25%. If you try to time the market and sell too early, you miss the upside—and in the process, shoot yourself in the foot. If you get back in too early or too late, you increase the odds of losing more and making less than your buy and hold peers.

Market timing is your enemy. It will damage your long-term returns and create unwarranted tax liability along the way. Avoid market timing and reduce the chances of shooting yourself in both feet. When clients ask me about market timing, I often respond with a quip based on the Forbes 400. Forbes magazine publishes an annual listing of the 400 wealthiest people in the world. "Warren Buffet has graced the cover of Forbes magazine several times as the wealthiest man in the world, yet not once have I seen a market timer in the top 400."

The big challenge with timing markets is the difficulty of knowing when to get back in after an initial sell. Investors watch early-stage bull markets slowly climb a wall of worry and pass them by awaiting the perfect re-entry point. Selling not only invites the opportunity to miss an entire upward move, but may also trigger capital gains taxes. This creates another significant disadvantage relative to the buy-and-hold investor. I truly believe the timeless adage: "It is time in rather than timing the market that makes investors rich."

Impulse Selling
Can Damage Performance
Performance of the S&P 500 Index, 1970-2013

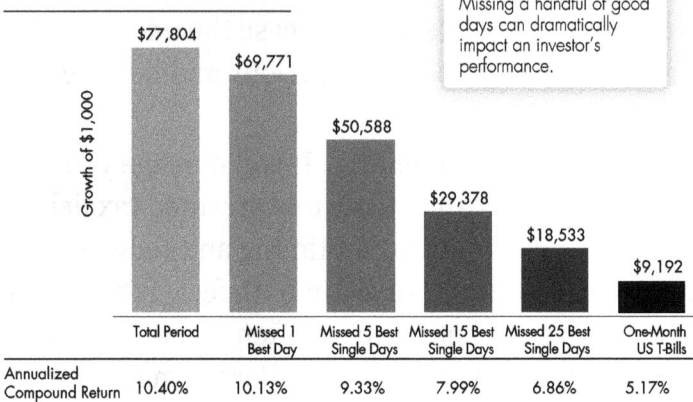

> Missing a handful of good days can dramatically impact an investor's performance.

	Total Period	Missed 1 Best Day	Missed 5 Best Single Days	Missed 15 Best Single Days	Missed 25 Best Single Days	One-Month US T-Bills
Growth of $1,000	$77,804	$69,771	$50,588	$29,378	$18,533	$9,192
Annualized Compound Return	10.40%	10.13%	9.33%	7.99%	6.86%	5.17%

This chart emphasizes the benefit of staying invested, even in tough markets.

A Study of Market Timing

Dimensional Fund Advisors is one of the premier fund management firms in the world. Driven by evidence based investing, they published a study on market timing in 2014. The study examines the impact of missing a small number of days over a 43 year time frame between 1970 and 2013. The results may shock you. Someone investing $1,000 into the index in 1973, reinvesting dividends and capital gains, grows their account to $77,804 by the end of 2013. An investor attempting to time the market, who misses the best 25 days, ends up with only $18,533. Missing less than one day per year over a 43-year time frame, costs more than $60,000 worth of growth on her original investment.

Focus on the Future, not your Fear

Humans are not wired for successful investing. Why? Because fear tends to take over when markets are falling, and greed steps in when markets are on a sustained upward run.

Investing is not a game; it's a way to create or sustain wealth and fund your future lifestyle. Market timing is a fool's game. Think of explaining it to your kids. "Kids, investing is for the long term, so don't listen to the talking heads on the news. Stay focused on the long term."

One final and compelling lesson I learned the hard way during the market crash in 1987: *Never, ever sell into a panic. Doing so destroys your return. Instead, buy when others are selling, and sell when others are buying. The concept of asset allocation encourages investors to do exactly that, which we will examine in the next chapter.*

RULE #7
MAINTAIN A BALANCED PORTFOLIO

Burton Malkiel, famous economist and author of *A Random Walk Down Wall Street*, is often quoted as saying, "The closest thing you get to a free lunch in the financial markets is diversification." Malkiel is a strong advocate of Nobel Prize-winning economist Dr. Eugene Fama's efficient-market hypothesis and agrees that low cost index funds serve investors best in the long run.

True diversification means more than owning stocks and bonds but owning them across the globe in large numbers. Utilizing low cost and highly diversified funds, my firm constructs portfolios with more than 10,000 distinctly different stocks and bonds issued by corporations and sovereign governments across the globe. With such diversity and given the randomness of returns, it is imperative to rebalance your portfolio at least once a year. Rebalancing is the essence of selling on strength and buying on weakness.

Diversification is an excellent tool for reducing risk. If you never rebalance your portfolio, key benefits of diversification are lost. Capital market data reveals that over long periods, stocks earn roughly 10% and bonds earn 6%. Simple arithmetic dictates stocks in your portfolio will become a larger percentage over time. As we all know, stock prices will drop dramatically from time to time. Failing to rebalance your portfolio increases the odds of large losses in a steep market decline. Rebalancing also creates a discipline for buying when prices are low.

Striking a Rebalance

Let's look at an example where stocks experienced a multi-year bull market such as the surging market of the late 1990s. Beginning in 1995 the S&P 500 stock index began a five-year run of double digit increases. The highest annual return of 37.6% came in 1995, and the lowest return of 21% came in 1999. Over that five-year cycle, an investor in the S&P 500 would have averaged close to a 30% annualized return!

Not so fast. We all know what happened when the tech bubble burst. The market giveth and the market taketh away. Annual rebalancing reduces gains in up markets and cushions against losses when markets fall. When the market taketh away, you will be happy you rebalanced.

Here's a simple example. A hypothetical investor is holding 60% in stocks and 40% in bonds at the beginning of a calendar year. Keep in mind it is not unusual for stocks to experience returns above 20% in any given year. Our investor sees her stock portfolio increase by 20% in the same year while her bonds stay flat and provide no return. ("Flat" is a Wall Street term meaning the asset class failed to increase in value.)

The following year, this same investor has a portfolio with more than 70% invested in stocks and less than 30% in bonds. She now has a riskier portfolio subject to sharper downturns and larger losses when the market moves lower. More stock market exposure equates to more risk and more personal pain in a downturn or correction.

In Wall Street speak, "correction" means stock prices are declining in value. Corrections become bear markets when a major index like the S&P 500 falls by more than 20%. When the S&P falls less than 20%, it is termed a correction. Corrections and Bear Markets highlight the need for restoring balance before a downturn arrives. Rebalancing is smart and helps you avoid unnecessary and unwanted risks.

Maintain Your Balance

The key in any portfolio is balance. Given that stocks tend to move up more than bonds over time, selling stocks and buying bonds is the usual method. In

Bear Markets it is time to turn the tables by selling bonds and buying stocks. It's smart and makes for a smoother ride and can even improve returns.

If your portfolio targets 60% stocks and 40% bonds, maintain that mix by rebalancing once per year. If your stocks have done well of late and you are adding money, look closely at your stock versus bond mix. Investing in bonds may just get you back on track. If bonds are rallying and stocks are dropping, invest new funds in stocks to maintain your targeted exposure. It is simple and it works. A good advisor will help you every step of the way.

These simple techniques can reduce risk and improve returns over longer periods. Remember, your goal should always be to rebalance back to your intended stock vs. bond exposure.

RULE #8
AVOID NOISE FROM THE MEDIA

Every form of media—written, spoken, print, or video—is in business to make a profit from advertisers. They are not in business to help you make a profit. CNBC, *Bloomberg News, The Nightly News, The New York Times, The Wall Street Journal, Forbes, Fortune, Money,* Twitter, Facebook, You Tube, and all the rest fund their operations through advertising.

Take a close at your preferred sources for investment news and information and then look at their primary advertisers. Likely you will see the same companies making money from your investments. Mutual Funds, On-Line Brokers, Insurance Companies and the like all want a few seconds of your attention. In short, they want your money and they are the fuel that drives the media engine.

Don't Believe Everything You See or Hear

Remember, the return of all investors must be the return of the market minus all fees and commissions. Financial media advertising channels investors' dollars to firms seeking fees or commissions. Given this simple yet profound truth, it pays to be circumspect when it comes to filtering your news sources.

I rely on the Wall Street Journal for background stories and general information. Bloomberg News works well for up to the minute market-related information and data. Neither is completely unbiased. All news, regardless of source, has some sort of spin. Jim Cramer is entertaining and I admire his success, yet do not rely on his guidance for investing. Jim is smart and certainly has made great calls during his broadcasting career. But he is no different than any other prognosticator—he has had his share of bad calls as well.

There are a few beacons in the media who have come to embrace the truth about investing. Jonathan Clements and Jason Zweig, both of the Wall Street Journal, are good examples. They're honest journalists who do their research and get it right. Larry Kudlow of CNBC stands out as level headed and concise.

Ignore the media and go direct to the source. Asset managers such as Dimensional Funds, Vanguard, and Blackrock are among the best. A consistent approach built upon academic research, low costs, and tax-efficient investing are hallmarks of all three providers. Yes, they make money from your investments but they do so with integrity.

Pay attention to how your favorite news sources make their money and choose wisely.

RULE #9
HIRE A FEE-BASED FINANCIAL ADVISOR

Find the Right Advisor

Do you do your own plumbing, fix your own electrical problems, pull your own teeth, or repair your own car? More than likely, you answered "no" to most of these questions. And it's likely you lack the skill or time necessary to be your own handyman, dentist, or mechanic. It is just as likely you lack the time and skill to manage your own investments. Smart investors hire experts to help make good decisions and track progress. Helping you stay the course during tough times is what good advisors do best.

Like any profession, the investment advisory business has good and bad practitioners. Finding a good fit for your needs poses a challenge. Think about how you found your favorite mechanic, electrician, dentist, or other professional. Chances are you found them the same way you will find the right financial advisor—by asking your friends and family. Your CPA or attorney, if you have one, can be a good source for finding a good financial advisor. Your CPA prepares tax returns for lots of clients. Inferior financial advisors will stand out. Skilled, successful advisors build superior reputations for delivering returns over market cycles. To be fair, every investor experiences losses from time to time. Inept advisors who routinely deliver poor results stand out in a CPA's client base. Estate planning attorneys with wealthy clientele always know the best financial advisors.

Involve Your Spouse

Selecting the right advisor is a process. It requires a time commitment from you and your spouse, if you have one. Always interview a prospective advisor with your spouse as an integral part of the process. I have been a financial advisor for three decades and several clients have passed away. The worst time for your spouse to meet your financial advisor is right after you die.

In the early days of my career, the boardroom at Merrill Lynch was filled with male clients. They'd drop off checks, chat with their brokers, and watch the old digital ticker go by. Times have changed—and investors are better off. Financial market data and portfolio tracking is easy with on line resources like Yahoo and Google to name a few but many people need help putting all the puzzle pieces together. Managing wealth and creating sound financial plans is serious business. In this age of two-career families, it is imperative to reach consensus when it comes to finances and investments. You and your spouse both need to respect and enjoy working with your advisor. All parties need to feel comfortable communicating honestly. Good chemistry between you and your advisor is the foundation for a successful, long-term relationship.

Advisors versus Brokers

The difference between advisors and brokers is simple yet profound. Registered investment advisors have a fiduciary duty to act in their clients' best interests at all times. Brokers, on the other hand, are only required to place their clients' money in investments that are "suitable." Suitability versus the fiduciary standard is a raging debate. The SEC, FINRA and other regulators are scrutinizing the industry for potential changes as this book goes to print. Suitability is a lower standard and can be rife with conflicts of interest. The fiduciary is held to a higher standard requiring full disclosure of all conflicts of interest.

The best advisors tend to be fee only, and many earn voluntary designations to set them apart from others in the industry. I prefer Accredited Investment Fiduciary (AIF) and Certified Financial Planner (CFP). Both designations require years of experience, months of study and rigorous exams. The AIF focuses on proper execution of fiduciary duties, stewardship, and the obligation to always act in a client's best interest. The CFP focuses on meeting educational standards related to every aspect of helping individuals manage and plan their finances. Both the AIF and CFP designations include ethical requirements, experience, and ongoing education.

These designations are evidence that an advisor has gone above and beyond to improve their skills. Other designations are attainable, but few have the weight of the AIF and the CFP. Investors should research and understand what those letters mean after a prospective advisor's name. Consider how much time you spend picking out a car that immediately depreciates after you buy it. Spend at least that amount of time selecting and interviewing the right advisor for you and your family.

The Value of an Advisor

The Vanguard Group studies the market performance of investors under the guidance of an advisor. The conclusion is that the right advisors add measurable value. Vanguard uses the trademarked term "Advisor's Alpha" to describe the added return that can come from working with a good advisor.

Solid portfolio structure, intelligent asset allocation, and reassurance during a market decline come with good advice. According to Vanguard, the potential to add three percentage points of return may come from working with the right advisor!

The Vanguard Group has offered investors access to some of the best index funds in the marketplace for over four decades. They are one of the largest and most respected fund managers in the world.

Vanguard's research indicates advisors help investors avoid damaging emotional mistakes during sharp market downturns. Good advisors are wealth managers and coaches. They can help you avoid harmful behavioral errors that destroy returns. Greed and fear are powerful and gripping emotions. Fear often undermines investors' long-term resolve during long bear markets and swift market declines.

My mother always used to say, "Experience is the best teacher but by far the most expensive." She was right. Selling at or near the bottom can be a poignant and painful lesson leading to fear of financial markets. You can visit vanguard.com for further insights on "Advisor's Alpha."

Good advisors are like good quarterbacks, good point guards, and good mid-fielders. They understand the chemistry of the team and bring out the best in the people around them. Intelligent wealth management includes assembling the right team. A smart CPA, experienced estate planning attorney and trustworthy insurance agent working in concert with your financial advisor will lead to better outcomes for you and your family.

Be smart and hire the right advisor for your family and your future. Ask around, make a few phone calls and interview a handful of candidates. A small investment of time may provide a lifetime of rewards.

RULE #10
THE SECRET TO SUCCESSFUL INVESTING

The secret to successful investing is you.

The nucleus of every successful plan, profitable portfolio, and inheritance passed down to the next generation is someone just like you with the self-discipline to save, the wisdom to invest, and the guts to hold on during tough times.

I hope you're ready to make the most of the secret to successful investing and I hope you're not disappointed. You control the amount you save. You determine how much to spend and where to invest. You are the one who rides through the ups and downs of the market.

Spend Less Than You Make

To become a successful investor, the first step is to spend less than you make. Spending less leaves more to invest. Remember: The borrower is always slave to the lender. For financial freedom, avoid using large amounts of credit whenever possible. Wealthy people do not carry balances on credit cards from month to month. Instead, they pay them off and pay cash for their big buys such as cars. Typically, they only borrow money to finance home purchases.

To avoid spending more than you make, create a budget and embark on a regular savings program. It's particularly important to convey this concept to your children. Make sure they know the secret to wealth is simply spending less than you make.

The more you save and the less you spend, the more wealth you create.

Establish an Emergency Fund

On your path to financial peace of mind, the first step is to establish an emergency fund. This fund pays for the unexpected car repair, the emergency room visit, or the leaky roof. It is not for Christmas presents, a family vacation, or the latest and greatest cell phone or big-screen TV. Have a fixed monthly amount taken out of your checking account and deposited automatically into a safe account.

It is smart to build up at least three times your monthly expenses in a risk-free vehicle like a savings account or a money market fund. Do not expose your emergency fund to the risks of either the stock or bond markets. Flee from any financial advisor who tells you a bond fund is a safe place to park your money. Savings accounts with a bank are excellent for your emergency fund. The Federal Deposit Insurance Corporation (FDIC) insures your account up to $250,000.00.

Protect Your Income Through Insurance

The next step is making sure you're properly insured. Basic health insurance protects more than your health; it protects your savings and investments. Medical bills are the number one cause of bankruptcy. Purchasing an inexpensive major medical policy can protect you from financial ruin.

Next, protect your income by securing basic disability insurance. An Internet search will lead to online resources about the nuts and bolts of buying a disability policy. Your family insurance agent who sells auto, renters', and life insurance is often a good resource. As with all insurance, shop around for the best rates and coverage.

Disability and life insurance are essential to protecting your wealth and your family. Spend time comparing rates and seek out reliable, trustworthy sources for the best types policies to hold. If you are just starting out, inexpensive term life and lower cost long-term disability are the better options.

Invest for the Long Term

Once the savings and insurance pieces of your puzzle are in place, it's time to begin the most crucial step toward building wealth: investing for the long term.

What's the big difference between saving and investing? You **save money** in a risk-free account and you **invest money** in a portfolio that involves taking risk. That's how you earn meaningful returns on the money you invest over time.

Risk and return are inseparable. Earning higher returns requires taking on the risk of temporary losses during down markets. Do not obsess over the daily performance of your investments. Leave your portfolio alone and focus only on long-term results.

Saving for Your Retirement

Where should you begin saving? That's a great question; let's delve into a few answers.

Most employers offer some type of retirement savings plan, which is a great place to begin investing for the long term. The most popular vehicle is called a 401(k) Plan. For folks in the nonprofit and public sectors, similar types of plans are referred to as a 403(b) or 457 Plan.

All these plans function in the same way and allow you, as an employee, to save part of your income for retirement. Often your employer matches some of your savings. Matching contributions can dramatically increase the compounding effect on your money over time. Many studies over the past decade suggest that American workers should save at least 10% of their pay for retirement. Most Americans do not start saving early and do not save enough. If you begin early and increase your savings rate every year by 1%, you'll be miles ahead of the pack.

No matter how old you are, start saving now. If your employer offers a match, you should invest the required percentage to capture those matching funds. It's like getting free money. Sit down with your human resource or payroll person right away to determine the match for your plan. Invest the proper percentage to capture every free dollar available. Regardless, start saving now. You will never miss 1% of your paycheck and that's a great place to begin. Increase your savings rate by 1% per year and you will be on track for a well-funded retirement.

Roth versus Traditional 401(k)

If your employer offers a Roth as well as Traditional 401(k) option, give the Roth close consideration. For workers under the age of 45 with 20 years until retirement, the Roth option will make a lot of sense over time. A Roth plan allows you to contribute after tax money to your 401(k) but will provide tax-free income in retirement. Do you think tax rates will increase in the future? If your answer is "yes" then take advantage of the Roth option in your 401(k) with some portion of your savings.

A Traditional 401(k) allows you to save a portion of your pay "pretax" and allows your investments to grow free from tax as well. That means you don't pay tax on the money you save from your paychecks. You also won't pay tax on the earnings inside a Traditional 401(k) Plan. The IRS provides no free lunches. You will pay taxes on all the money distributed to you later in life from a Traditional 401(k).

A Roth 401(k) plan allows you to save money after tax and your savings compound free from tax along the way. Unlike a Traditional 401(k) Plan, income distributed from a Roth plan in retirement is free from tax. Tax-free income later in life is a powerful benefit; so give the Roth option close consideration.

For younger workers, the Roth 401(k) savings plan makes a lot of sense, especially if the tax code does not change. Choosing to invest in a Roth versus a Traditional 401(k) Plan is a major decision. Seeking credible advice from a CPA or investment advisor is a wise move.

Find a Good Financial Advisor

Financial decisions are often complex and cry out for expert insights. How much to save and where to invest in your company retirement plan are big decisions. Navigating this maze points to the need for hiring a fee-only financial advisor with a solid reputation. Even if you aren't making a lot of money, find a good advisor who charges hourly fees and offers sound advice on personal finances. Rule #9 explores the advantages of working with a fee-based advisor.

Let's do a quick inventory. At this point your emergency fund is in set up and your retirement savings are on autopilot. Next, proper life and disability insurance coverage's are in place. Finally it is time start your personal investment plan for building wealth.

Choose Wisely Today to Build Wealth for Your Future

Wealth is nothing more than "the condition of having a surplus" Being wealthy means having more than you need to survive and provides more security and freedom to choose a lifestyle.

Attaining wealth **always** begins with you and **always** requires self-discipline. Simply spending less than you make—and investing those funds—produces powerful, long-lasting results.

Wise choices today are the building blocks for a secure and abundant future. I hope your current notion of personal responsibility and your sense of how to create a better future are soundly in place.

Regardless of where you are today, start your wealth creation plan now. You control your finances. Begin building a team of experts tomorrow to help create, grow, and protect your assets over time. Your peace of mind in the future depends on the little things you do every day. Regardless of where you are on the journey, start now to make your future bigger and better than your past.

FINAL THOUGHTS

Focus on what is truly important in your life. Practice self-discipline. Tune out the noise of the media. Set goals, and the results will exceed your wildest expectations.

The secret to investing, like so many questions in life, lies within. I wish you many blessings on your personal pathway to wealth. A new lesson arrives each day and the opportunity for learning never ends.

⬤ MY PATHWAY

My Pathway is a revolutionary
service bridging the gap
between traditional financial
advice and web based
portfolio management.

www.2Mypathway.com

Pathways
FINANCIAL PARTNERS

Pathways Financial Partners
is a Registered Investment
Advisor and full service
Wealth Management firm
based in Tucson, Arizona.
Brian and his team at
Pathways specialize in
helping clients implement
proven portfolio strategies
based on academic principles
in conjunction with long
range planning. Pathways
process is transparent,
honest, and individually
tailored to each client.

www.2Pathways.com